P9-DJK-544

MOVIE MAKERS

PETER JACKSON

Director of The Lord of the Rings and The Hobbit Trilogies

Rebecca Felix

Checkerboard
Library

An Imprint of Abdo Publishing
abdopublishing.com

ABDOPUBLISHING.COM

Published by Abdo Publishing, a division of ABDO, PO Box 398166, Minneapolis, Minnesota 55439. Copyright © 2017 by Abdo Consulting Group, Inc. International copyrights reserved in all countries. No part of this book may be reproduced in any form without written permission from the publisher. Checkerboard Library™ is a trademark and logo of Abdo Publishing.

Printed in the United States of America, North Mankato, Minnesota

062016
092016

THIS BOOK CONTAINS RECYCLED MATERIALS

Design: Christa Schneider, Mighty Media, Inc.
Production: Mighty Media, Inc.
Editor: Paige Polinsky
Cover Photograph: AP Images
Interior Photographs: Alamy, p. 13, 28; AP Images, pp. 5, 9, 19, 21, 22, 29; Everett Collection NYC, pp. 17, 25; Getty Images, pp. 15, 27; Shutterstock, pp. 7, 11, 28; Wikimedia Commons, p. 19

Publishers Cataloging-in-Publication Data

Names: Felix, Rebecca, author.
Title: Peter Jackson : director of the Lord of the Rings and the Hobbit trilogies / by Rebecca Felix.
Description: Minneapolis, MN : Abdo Publishing, [2017] | Series: Movie makers | Includes index.
Identifiers: LCCN 2016934267 | ISBN 9781680781823 (lib. bdg.) | ISBN 9781680775679 (ebook)
Subjects: LCSH: Jackson, Peter, 1961- --Juvenile literature. | Motion picture producers and directors--New Zealand--Biography--Juvenile literature. | Screenwriters--New Zealand--Biography--Juvenile literature.
Classification: DDC 791.4302/33/092 [B]--dc23
LC record available at /http://lccn.loc.gov/2016934267

CONTENTS

A WORLD OF SUCCESS

Across Middle Earth, elves live in secret tree castles. Goblins, dwarves, and humans unite against a rising evil. Wizards battle for power. This is the world of The Lord of the Rings (LOTR). It is one of the most successful film series of all time.

Peter Jackson is the man behind these amazing films. Jackson is a **screenwriter**, **producer**, and **director**. He turned author J.R.R. Tolkien's beloved LOTR **trilogy** into three successful films. The undertaking took about eight years. During this time, director Jackson led thousands of actors and crew members.

Jackson's vision took great **dedication**. And the result of his hard work was three smash hits. Altogether, the films and their **cast** and crew were nominated for more than 250 awards!

Peter Jackson stands in front of a troll model from his LOTR films. The effects company Weta Workshop created this and 48,000 other items for the series.

CHAPTER 2

ADVENTURE AND ANIMATION

eter Robert Jackson was born on October 31, 1961, in Wellington, New Zealand. He was raised in nearby Pukerua Bay. The small coastal town was full of beauty. Its ocean, forests, and hills would later inspire Peter's interpretation of Middle Earth.

Peter was the only child of Bill and Joan Jackson. Bill was a payroll clerk, and Joan stayed at home. Joan was an excellent storyteller, and made up stories just for Peter. Peter also spent much time reading on his own. He imagined the books' fantasies taking place in his hometown.

When Peter was five, the Jacksons bought their first television. Peter liked watching the science-fiction show *Thunderbirds*. It featured **special effects**, puppets, and **stop-motion**. Peter re-created **scenes** from the show with his toy cars.

Jackson later described Wellington, New Zealand, as "an adventure playground." Its scenery greatly influenced his film career.

Peter enjoyed watching movies too. At age nine, he watched the 1933 film *King Kong*. The movie used **special effects** to bring a model of a giant gorilla to life. Peter loved it! He wanted to make his own films. The next morning, he began doing just that.

Recently, a family friend had noticed that Peter loved taking photos. So, she gave him a **super 8mm** movie camera. Peter now used that camera to film his own **stop-motion** "King Kong." The short film was the first of many movie projects.

Peter's parents supported his filmmaking. They let Peter take over the kitchen to create **props**. Joan even helped him bake model heads made out of foam **latex**! Sometimes the family skipped their Sunday night roast so that Peter could use the oven for his models.

Peter created his own **sets** and **special effects**. He and his friends acted in the films together. They created one movie to raise funds for a class trip. The short film was played in their school's assembly hall for ten cents per ticket. Peter had discovered his calling as a **director**.

MAGIC ACT

Peter quickly began experimenting with camera tricks. His first special effect was making a cat disappear. He also made one of his teachers vanish while opening an umbrella. By poking holes in his film, he could fake the flash of gunfire. Peter used these special effects and more in his movies.

Jackson displays the King Kong model he created in 1973.
His childhood remake of the film used a cardboard Empire
State Building.

CHAPTER 3

FULL-TIME FILMMAKER

Jackson continued making films into his teen years. At age 16, he left school. He wanted to earn money for film equipment. Jackson took a job at the local newspaper. After two years, he had saved up enough money for a better camera.

At age 22, Jackson began making *Bad Taste*, a science-fiction horror film. After about four years of filming, the New Zealand Film Commission (NZFC) heard about *Bad Taste*. Jim Booth, the commission **chairman**, liked the film. In 1986, the NZFC gave Jackson $235,000 for filming and editing. Jackson quit his newspaper job to focus on the movie.

FAST FACT

Jackson played the lead role in his film *Bad Taste*. He also built all the models used in the film.

The Cannes Film Festival began in 1946. Today it is one of the most well-known film festivals in the world.

In 1988, Jackson entered *Bad Taste* in the esteemed Cannes Film Festival. It was a hit! Jackson made deals to **distribute** the film in 12 countries. He then signed into a partnership with Booth.

Jackson not only found success while making *Bad Taste*. He also found love! Jackson worked with **screenwriter** Fran Walsh to finish the film. The couple married in 1987.

CHAPTER 4

FEAR AND FANTASY

During the early 1990s, Jackson and Booth made several movies together. Jackson especially enjoyed making horror films, such as 1992's *Dead Alive*. He was also very interested in **special effects**.

In 1993, Jackson created the company Weta Digital. It was a digital special effects company based in New Zealand. The next year, Jackson teamed up with his friends Richard Taylor and Tania Rodger. Together they expanded Taylor and Rodger's special effects studio to form Weta Workshop. It created **props**, makeup effects, costumes, and more for the entertainment industry.

Jackson was also busy at home as his family grew. In 1995, he and Fran welcomed their first child, Billy. Their daughter Katie was born the next year. Jackson and Fran continued making films while raising their children.

Weta Workshop has provided visual effects for more than 70 movies and television series. The company has won 35 awards, including five Academy Awards.

Meanwhile, Weta Workshop continued to create special effects for films. Its **technology** had greatly improved. Now Jackson wanted Weta to create over-the-top effects for a major film.

Fran shared Jackson's vision. But the two had trouble inventing a **plot**. They wanted an exciting story with battles, swordplay, and monsters. Jackson and Fran wished they could turn Tolkien's LOTR books into a movie.

In 1995, Jackson and Fran looked into making their dream a reality. **Producer** Saul Zaentz owned the LOTR film rights. Zaentz had made an **animated** LOTR film in the 1970s. But it only combined stories from the first two books. This upset Tolkien fans, who expected to see the entire **trilogy**.

In 1997, film company Miramax helped Jackson obtain the LOTR film rights. Jackson planned to turn the books into two films. But after writing the scripts, he was met with bad news. The film company wanted to combine the movies. Jackson refused, knowing he would have to cut too much out of the story.

FAST FACT

Author J.R.R. Tolkien spent 14 years writing The Lord of the Rings. The trilogy has sold more than 150 million copies.

Saul Zaentz felt his own LOTR films couldn't fully capture Tolkien's story. He believes the trilogy was "too complex for [animation] to handle it."

Jackson took the project to another studio, New Line **Cinema**. New Line agreed, but asked Jackson to make three movies! The studio also allowed Jackson to film all three at once. If the first movie failed, New Line would not be able to cancel the others. But the studio's executives trusted Jackson's ability and vision.

ARMIES OF ACTORS

Jackson chose New Zealand as the setting for all three LOTR films. He felt the country's scenery was perfect for the story. He also wanted Weta Workshop to create the film's **special effects.**

Jackson chose actors carefully. Filming the **trilogy** all at once made the final **cast** permanent. But Jackson felt the team was perfect. "Everybody showed up on **set** every day with a spirit of, 'Let's make this as good as it can be,'" he said.

Jackson had spent three years writing and planning. Filming began on October 11, 1999. The LOTR team was now ready for three years of acting, filming, and fun!

FAST FACT

Jackson's children, Billy and Katie, acted in the LOTR series. The first film's credits list them each as "Cute **Hobbit** Child."

Warriors of Gondor and Rohan prepare to fight in *LOTR: The Return of the King.* It is the final major battle in the series.

ON THE SET OF
THE LORD OF THE RINGS

One news publication called The Lord of the Rings "the most ambitious film production ever attempted at that time." Jackson employed up to 20,000 people during filming. This included about 10,000 **extras**!

The extras acted in the films' huge battle **scenes**. These scenes included thousands of **props** too. Overall, there were more than 48,000 pieces of armor and 19,000 costumes used in the films. Weta Workshop created all of these items, as well 3,200 fake **hobbit** feet!

Even while **directing** a **cast** of thousands, Jackson kept the **sets** relaxed and fun. He also made sure the films followed the books closely.

FAST FACT

Jackson wore the same two shirts and same pair of shoes during the entire LOTR filming.

Peter Jackson (*second from right*) directs actor Sean Bean (*right*) on the set of *LOTR: The Two Towers*. Bean plays the character Boromir in the films.

The Hobbiton movie set in Waikato, New Zealand, is now a major tourist location. Visitors can take guided tours and eat at The Shire's Rest Café.

Before each **scene**, the entire team would reread that portion of the book. Sometimes Jackson even acted them out himself.

It took eight years to finish the LOTR series. Of those eight years, the actual filming lasted only 274 days. By the end, Jackson had created a special bond between his **cast** and crew. He had also created three very special films!

BOX-OFFICE
BOOM

CHAPTER
6

The Fellowship of the Ring was released in 2001. The first film in the **trilogy** was an immediate success! Fans were thrilled with the film's representation of the book. The movie also created many new LOTR fans who hadn't read Tolkien's series.

Critics liked the film too. It received 13 **Academy Award**, or Oscar, nominations! Fans, critics, and the **cast** and crew anxiously awaited the next release.

When *The Two Towers* came out in 2002, it was another smash hit. The third and final film, *The Return of the King*, was released the next year. *The Return of the King* made more than $1 billion during its release. This made it the

FAST FACT

Jackson's favorite LOTR film is *The Two Towers*. He enjoys the fact that it jumps right into the story.

Actor Christopher Lee as the wizard Saruman in *The Fellowship of the Ring*. In one interview, Lee said, "This film is a modern miracle and it will be remembered for a long, long time."

Fran Walsh (*left*) and Peter Jackson carry Oscars won for their work on *The Return of the King*.

twelfth highest-earning film of all time. Fans and **critics** praised it as the strongest in the series.

In 2004, *The Return of the King* won 11 **Oscars**. This tied the record for most awards won by a single film. Jackson and Walsh won an Oscar for Best Adapted Screenplay. Jackson also won an Oscar for Best **Director**.

The LOTR series was nominated for hundreds of awards, and it won many. The three films made $3 billion at the **box office.** The Lord of the Rings was called the most successful film series in history. Jackson had fulfilled his dream in big way.

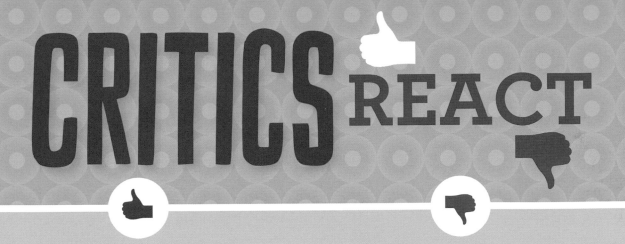

CRITICS REACT

"Peter Jackson's movie is a piece of wonderment beyond anything crafted for the cinema in a long time. On all fronts it is the movie of the year, and, really, people who don't like this movie in some fundamental way just don't like the movies."

—Andrew O'Hagan,
The Daily Telegraph

"They eviscerated the book by making it an action movie for young people. . . . What [Tolkien's work] has become, has overwhelmed me. . . . There is only one solution for me: to turn my head away."

—Christopher Tolkien,
son of The Lord of the Rings
author J.R.R. Tolkien

The writers both reviewed *The Lord of the Rings: The Fellowship of the Ring,* but their opinions are very different. Consider both sides. Who makes a better argument? Do you agree with one review more than the other? Why?

KING KONG, HOBBITS,

CHAPTER 7

AND HOME

In 2003, film studio Universal Pictures asked Jackson to re-create the very movie that inspired his career. Universal Pictures hired him to remake *King Kong*. The studio gave Jackson $20 million for **special effects**.

Like LOTR, *King Kong* was filmed in New Zealand. And much of the film's creation relied on Weta Workshop. A large team of computer **animators** worked to create the film's giant gorilla.

MONSTER STAR

Actor Andy Serkis played King Kong in Jackson's remake. During filming, Serkis had small sensors attached to his body. These sensors transferred his movements to the computer-animated gorilla.

Jackson speaks with actor Jack Black on the set of *King Kong*. The film became one of the highest-selling home videos ever made.

King Kong's 2005 release was a great success. Later, the film's home-video sales soared. The remake made Jackson the highest paid **director** in film history!

After ten years of major projects, Jackson took a break from directing. But he remained involved in moviemaking. Weta Digital worked on several major films, including 2009's science-fiction *Avatar*. In 2010, Jackson was named a Knight Companion of the Order, New Zealand's highest honor.

It wasn't long before Jackson returned to Middle Earth. He turned *The **Hobbit***, Tolkien's LOTR **prequel**, into three films. The first, *The Hobbit: An Unexpected Journey*, released in 2012. *The Hobbit: The **Desolation** of Smaug* came out in 2013. The final film, *The Hobbit: The Battle of the Five Armies*, released in 2014.

Like the LOTR series, the Hobbit films were filmed in New Zealand. And all three were wildly successful. Viewers were excited to watch Jackson interpret another Tolkien classic.

FAST FACT

Jackson's mansion in New Zealand has an exact copy of an underground hobbit home from his films! People have to go through tunnels to reach this part of Jackson's house.

Jackson leaves a hobbit hole at the 2012 premiere of *The Hobbit: An Unexpected Journey* in Wellington, New Zealand. The film was nominated for three Oscars in 2013.

Jackson created a world of success right from home. Today, he and Fran live in Wellington, New Zealand. Weta Digital is the world's top provider of digital **special effects**. Jackson's vision has brought amazing worlds to life for millions of fans.

TIMELINE

1961

Peter Jackson is born on October 31 in Wellington, New Zealand.

1970

Jackson watches 1933's *King Kong*. The movie inspires him to become a filmmaker.

1986

The New Zealand Film Commission funds Jackson's first full-length film, *Bad Taste*.

1987

Peter Jackson and Fran Walsh are married.

1988

Jackson releases *Bad Taste* at the Cannes Film Festival.

1993

Jackson cofounds digital effects company Weta Digital.

FAMOUS WORKS

LOTR: *The Fellowship of the Ring*
Released 2001

Jackson appears in one scene, outside the Prancing Pony inn.

Won: Best Cinematography, Academy Awards, 2002

LOTR: *The Two Towers*
Released 2002

This movie made nearly $1 billion worldwide.

Won: Movie of the Year, American Film Awards, 2003

LOTR: *The Return of the King*
Released 2003

Jackson considers this film "the most special" of the three.

Won: Best Director, Academy Awards, 2004

FAST FACT

Weta Workshop built nearly 800 weapons for *An Unexpected Journey*'s 13 dwarves.

1995
Jackson and Fran's son, Billy, is born.

1996
Jackson and Fran's daughter, Katie, is born.

1999
Jackson begins filming *The Fellowship of the Ring*, the first in the LOTR trilogy.

2004
Jackson wins the Academy Award for Best Director for his work on *The Return of the King*.

2005
Jackson's *King Kong* remake is released.

2010
Jackson is named a Knight Companion of the Order.

King Kong
Released 2005

King Kong's roar was created by playing a slowed-down lion's roar backward.

Won: Movie of the Year, American Film Awards, 2006

The Hobbit: An Unexpected Journey
Released 2012

It took 18 months for Jackson and Walsh to write the script.

Won: Best Sci-Fi/Fantasy, Empire Awards, UK, 2013

The Hobbit: The Desolation of Smaug
Released 2013

This is the only Tolkien film missing the character Frodo.

Won: Best Fight, MTV Movie Awards, 2014

GLOSSARY

Academy Award – one of several awards the Academy of Motion Picture Arts and Sciences gives to the best actors and filmmakers of the year.

animation – a process involving a projected series of drawings that appear to move due to slight changes in each drawing. An *animator* is a person who creates a work using this process.

box office – income from ticket sales of a movie or a play. Also, a booth or an office where tickets for a movie or a play are sold.

cast – the actors in a play, movie, or television program.

chairman – a person who is in charge of a committee, a company, or a department in a school.

cinema – the movie industry.

critic – a professional who gives his or her opinion on art, literature, or performances.

dedication – a commitment to a goal or a way of life.

desolation – a state of total destruction.

direct – to supervise people in a play, movie, or television program. Someone who directs is a *director*.

distribute – to make something available to a number of people or different places.

eviscerate – to remove a vital part of something.

extra – a person hired to act in a group scene in a movie or a play.

hobbit – a small, fictional, human-like creature who lives underground.

WEBSITES

To learn more about Movie Makers, visit booklinks.abdopublishing.com. These links are routinely monitored and updated to provide the most current information available.

latex – a mixture of water and tiny particles of rubber.

Oscar – see *Academy Award*.

plot – the main story of a novel, movie, play, or any work of fiction.

prequel – a movie or book that tells the part of a story that happened before the story in another movie or book.

producer – someone who oversees staff and funding to put on a play or make a movie or TV show.

prop – any item other than costumes or furniture that appears in a play, movie, or television show.

scene – a part of a play, movie, or TV show that presents what is happening in one particular place and time.

screenwriter – a person who writes the story and directions for a movie.

sensor – an instrument that can detect, measure, and transmit information to a controlling device.

set – an artificial setting where a play is performed or a movie or television program is filmed.

special effects – visual or sound effects used in a movie or television program.

stop-motion – a filmmaking technique in which objects are photographed in a series of slightly different positions so that the objects seem to move.

super 8mm – a film format used in a type of home movie camera.

technology – the use of science to invent useful things or solve problems.

trilogy – a series of three novels, movies, or other works that are closely related and involve the same characters or themes.

INDEX